IN THE EYES OF THE CAT

Japanese Poetry for All Seasons

Selected and illustrated by

DEMI

Translated by Tze-si Huang

HARCOURT BRACE & COMPANY

Orlando   Atlanta   Austin   Boston   San Francisco   Chicago   Dallas   New York
Toronto   London

The Cat's Eye

In the eyes of the cat
Is the color of the sea,
On a sunny day, in winter.

—*Yorie, 1884–1941*

Morning Horses

O look!
See the horses
In the morning snow!

—*Bashō, 1644–94*

The Winter Cat

In the winter storm
The cat keeps on
Blinking its eyes.

—*Yasō*, seventeeth century

Ravens

A white heron on the snow
Is hard to see.
But the ravens
How they stand out!

—*Poet unknown*

The Egrets

That flight of egrets—
If they didn't cry—
Would be a streak of snow
Across the sky.

—Sōkan, 1458–1586

Weasel

Mandarin ducks;
A weasel peeping
At the old pond.

—Buson, 1715–83

Twilight

Snowfall at twilight,
Yet a mandarin drake and duck
Still linger
On the ancient lake.

—*Shiki, 1867–1902*

The Deer on the Mountain

Three times it cried
And was heard no more—
The voice of the deer.

—*Buson, 1715–83*

The Hare

The hail comes beating down;
A frightened hare bursts from the reeds
And dashes over ground!

—*Poet unknown*

Same and Different

The herons on the snow,
They are not the same;
The bright moon on the reeds,
They are not alike.

—*Poet unknown*

The Cat

Flourishing his head around,
He licks himself smooth and sleek—
The moonlight cat!

—*Kusatao, 1901–83*

Idea

The long night;
The monkey thinks how
To catch hold of the moon.

—*Shiki, 1867–1902*

Dawn

The little kitten's face
Like the sudden dawn
Swallows all of midnight
With a big pink yawn.

—*Poet unknown*

SPRING

The Lark's Song

The lark sings in heaven,
Sings on earth,
Sings as it rises.

—*Seisensui, 1884–1976*

The Mole's Work

Early dawn, the violets tilt—
Underneath, a home is built.

—*Bonchō, ?–1714*

The Cow's Moo

Here comes the cow
Moo! Moo!
Out of the mist.

—Issa, 1763–1827

In the Mist

In the depths of the mist
The horses nuzzle
Each other.

—*Seisensui, 1884–1976*

The Frog

Breaking the silence
Of an ancient pond,
A frog jumps in—
Plop!

—*Bashō, 1644–94*

Little Fish

Early dawn;
Young white fish
Shining in emerald white,
Hardly an inch long.

—*Bashō, 1644–94*

Nightingale

The little nightingale
Of buff and brown
Sings its first note
Upside down!

—*Kikaku, 1661–1707*

Nightingale's Feet

On white plum petals
That were pure and sweet,
The nightingale now
Wipes its muddy feet.

—Issa, 1763–1827

Mice

Mice in their nest
Squeak in response
To the young sparrows.

—Bashō, 1644–94

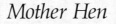

Mother Hen

The mother hen
Lets the chicks play
Among the hollyhocks.

—*Seibi, 1748–1816*

Innocence

The newborn foal
With knock-kneed pose
Above the irises
Pokes out his nose.

—Issa, 1763–1827

Puppy

Under the willow
With a leaf stuck in his mouth
The puppy sleeps.

—*Issa, 1763–1827*

The Little Duck

The little duck looks very wise
When he pops up fresh from the sight
Of what lies far below the water.

—Jōsō, 1663–1704

The Kingfisher

The kingfisher
Uses the pond as a mirror
To plume his wings so gay.

—*Poet unknown*

Young Calves

How cool the young calves seem!
They love to swish their tails and stand
Knee-deep in the stream.

—Banko, ?–1724

Mother Horse

A mother horse
Keeps watch
While her child
Drinks.

—*Issa, 1763–1827*

Finches

So much life in so few inches:
A perch of hopping, chirping, spotted finches!

—*Hō-ō, ?–1798*

Energy

The frog
Rises up by the same force
With which it jumps in.

—*Tōrei, 1638–1719*

Busy

Little gray cuckoos
Sing and sing! Fly and fly!
Oh, so much to do!

—*Bashō, 1644–94*

Doves

Although I saw you
The day before yesterday,
And yesterday and today,
This much is true—
I want to see you tomorrow too!

—*Masahito*, eighth century A.D.

The Black Bull

Under this plum tree,
Even a black bull will learn
To sing a joyful song of spring.

—Bashō, 1644–94

Foxes

The foxes
Are playing hide-and-seek
In the flowers
Of early moonlight.

—*Buson, 1715–83*

SUMMER

Joyful Crickets

O leaping crickets,
Watch what you do!
You might land and split
These emeralds of dew.

—Issa, 1763–1827

Ladybird

The ladybird flies off,
Dividing her wings
Into two.

—*Sujū, 1893–1976*

Garter Snake

The garter snake
Goes in and out of the grass
At the same time!

—*Poet unknown*

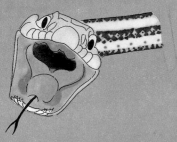

Snake Eyes

The snake slid away,
But the eyes that glared at me
Remained in the grass.

—*Kyōshi, 1874–1959*

Unseen till Now

How visibly
The gentle morning airs
Stir in the caterpillar's
Silky hairs.

—Buson, 1715–83

The Snail

The snail sticks out his horns.
Oh, see! Eyes like shining drops of dew
Upon the ends has he!

—*Ransetsu, 1654–1707*

The Reader

This butterfly
Which on a poppy clings
Opens, shuts
Its book of tiny paper wings.

—*Buson, 1715–83*

Dreams of Flowers

If butterflies
Could only speak,
What pretty dreams
We'd have about the flowers!

—*Reikan*, dates unknown

The Swan

The white swan, swimming
To the shore beyond,
Parts with his breast
The cherry-petaled pond.

—*Rōka, 1669–1703*

In the Forest

The little fawn
So slim and light
Finds lacy vines
His bed for night.

—*Poet unknown*

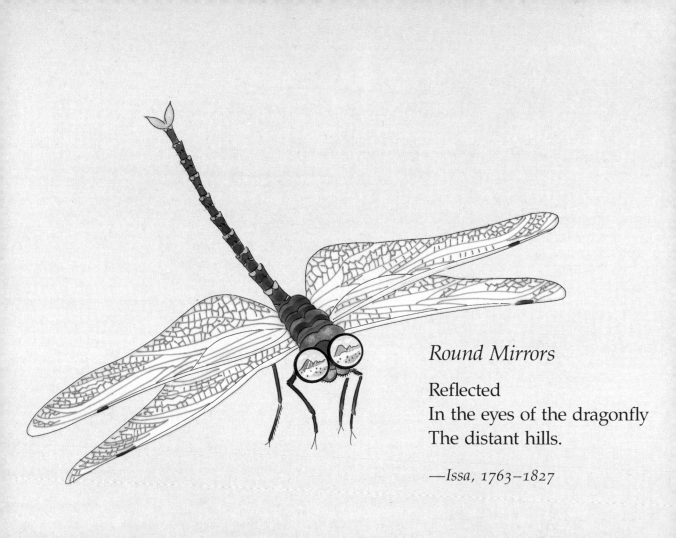

Round Mirrors

Reflected
In the eyes of the dragonfly
The distant hills.

—Issa, 1763–1827

The Red Dragonfly

Add some wings to a pepper pod that's red
And you'll have
A red dragonfly instead.

—*Bashō, 1644–94*

The Catch

The kingfisher
On its wet feathers
Shines in the sun!

—*Tōri, ?–1779*

The Kitten

The kitten is playing
Hide-and-seek
Among the flowers.

—Issa, 1763–1827

Traveler

Where can he be going
In the rain,
This snail?

—Issa, 1763–1827

The Mud Snail

The mud snail
Crawls two or three feet—
And the day is over.

—*Gomei, 1730–1803*

Crabs

As I walk along,
All the crabs
Hide in the rushes!

—*Seishi, 1901—*

Nothing at All

Doing nothing at all,
The sea slug has lived
For eighteen thousand years.

—*Shiki, 1867–1902*

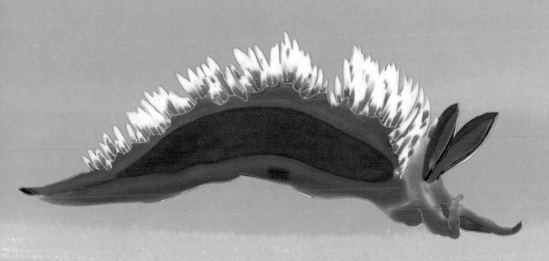

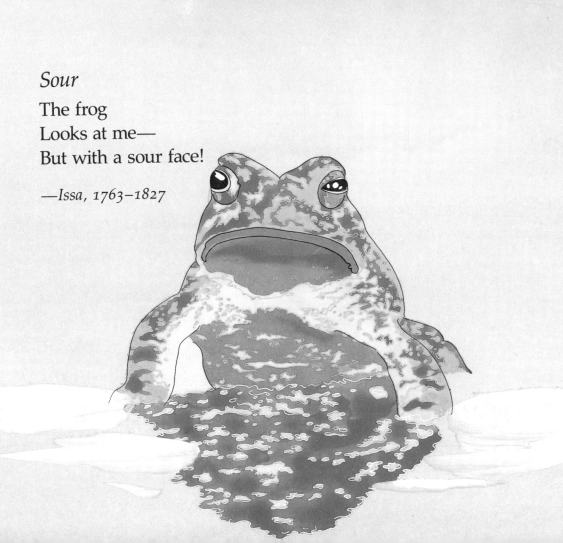

Sour

The frog
Looks at me—
But with a sour face!

—*Issa, 1763–1827*

The Petal

A petal lightly dropped
Upon the mouth of Mr. Frog,
And now his song is stopped.

—Ryūkyō, ?–1748

The Pheasant

The sun is setting
On the tail
Of the copper pheasant.

—Buson, 1715–83

Gnats

The sun set on the swamp
With an orange glare.
Look! There's a ball of gnats
Revolving in the air!

—*Poet unknown*

The Cicada

The silence!
The voice of the cicada
Penetrates the rocks!

—Bașhō, 1644–94

Meteor

Just as that firefly
Glowing on a spray of leaves
Dropped off—
It suddenly shot away!

—*Bashō, 1644–94*

Worm

At midnight
Under the bright moon,
A secret worm
Digs into a chestnut.

—*Bashō, 1644–94*

Broken Mirror

The full moon
On the water sits.
Mother hen
Pecks it into bits.

—Zuiryū, 1548–1628

The Night Owl

The midday sky
Is never seen
By the midnight owl.

—*Poet unknown*

Don't Come Out

Lizard!
If only you wouldn't come out—
You frighten me!

—*Raizan, 1653–1716*

AUTUMN

Kitten

The kitten
Holds down a leaf
For a moment.

—Issa, 1763–1827

Autumn

The puppy
That doesn't know
That autumn has come
Is happy!

—*Issa, 1763–1827*

The Cricket

In a sorrowful voice
A cricket is heard
Singing beneath
The withered grass.

—Bashō, 1644–94

Rabbits

Where can the rabbits play
In safety from the chestnut burs
That fall so fast today?

—*Seibi, 1748–1816*

Monkey

Out of a tree
Through which the wind beat
Tumbled a monkey
With a red seat.

—*Kyōtai, 1723–93*

Surprise

A pheasant flew up
And startled us
On the withered moor!

—Issa, 1763–1827

The Crow

A crow
Flew by
In silence.

—*Santōka, 1882–1940*

The Cuckoo

The voice of the cuckoo
Dropped to the lake,
Where it lay floating
On the surface.

—Bashō, 1644–94

The Mouse

A mouse is
Crossing a puddle
In the autumn tempest.

—*Buson, 1715–83*

Wild Boars

The autumn tempest
Blows along
Even wild boars.

—*Bashō, 1644–94*

The Sound

The sound of the bats
Flying in the thicket
Is dark.

—*Shiki, 1867–1902*

A Desolate Scene

The end of autumn
And a crow
Is perched upon a withered branch.

—Bashō, 1644–94

The Wild Goose

Faraway and faint
The wild goose gives his cry.
Since then my thoughts have been fixed
On the middle of the sky.

—*Misune*, tenth century A.D.

Winter Monkey

In the first storm
Of winter,
Even the monkey seems to want
A warm snowsuit.

—*Bashō, 1644–94*

This edition is published by special arrangement with Henry Holt and Company, Inc.

Grateful acknowledgment is made to Henry Holt and Company, Inc. for permission to reprint *In the Eyes of the Cat: Japanese Poetry for All Seasons*, selected and illustrated by Demi, translated by Tze-si Huang.
Copyright © 1992 by Demi.

Printed in the United States of America

ISBN 0-15-302163-2

4 5 6 7 8 9 10   035   97 96 95